THE SEX OF ART

Shearsman Library Vol. 7

Selected previous publications by Frances Presley

The Sex of Art
Hula-Hoop
Linocut
Neither the One nor the Other, *with Elizabeth James*
Automatic Cross Stitch, *with Irma Irsara*
Somerset Letters
Paravane
Myne *
Lines of sight *
Stone settings, *with Tilla Brading*
An Alphabet for Alina, *with Peterjon Skelt*
Halse for hazel *
Sallow

* Shearsman titles

Frances Presley

THE SEX OF ART

Shearsman Library

Second Edition.
Published in the United Kingdom in 2018 by
Shearsman Library
an imprint of Shearsman Books
50 Westons Hill Drive
Emersons Green
BRISTOL
BS16 7DF

Shearsman Books Ltd Registered Office
30–31 St. James Place, Mangotsfield, Bristol BS16 9JB
(this address not for correspondence)

www.shearsman.com

ISBN 978-1-84861-594-6

ACKNOWLEDGEMENTS
First published in 1987 by North and South,
Twickenham & Wakefield.

CONTENTS

AMERICA

HEROES OF OUR TIME

THE RIGHT BALANCE

GERMANY IN AUTUMN

THE COMMUNITY PROJECT

THE SEX OF ART

HOLLAND : ITHACA

THE SEX OF ART

AMERICA

PENNSYLVANIA WILDERNESS

Coming down to the Susquehanna
through the burnished gaming forests
of late Fall
I saw youth
with an outdated headband
poised in the wind of an outstretched rock
"Are you the new ghost of the Susquehanna?"
I inquired with sly hope

But the smile as his head turned around
was empty
and he asked us only for fresh water

BIRMINGHAM, ALABAMA

Three days of paranoia
a loaded gun always at hand
I lay against the crinkled grass
of a Jewish grave
because the black neighbourhood
was forbidden
The state of siege is alleviated
when my aunt allows me out to the library

Where
a host of multicoloured children
gabble like Thanksgiving turkeys at story time
or flap their wings
like fabled eagles together

In Atlanta I waited an hour while the 3038 bus was serviced to complete the last stage of its journey. I was one of only three people left since New York. Two elderly men occupied the front seats. One travelled considerably, the other said he didn't travel anymore because the changes would depress him too much. After something close to eternity the city lights and illuminated smoke of Birmingham extended below us and Vulcan raised his ominous greeting. The torch which so often burns red not green – signalling the road deaths in the previous twenty four hours. Just outside Birmingham there is a highway warning which takes the form of successive signs:

LOOK
WHAT WE
PICKED UP

a heap of tangled car wreckage lies dumped in the central reservation.

"Say hello to your aunt for me," said the black G.I., who sat next to me for twenty eight hours and left in Atlanta. Later I was shown the church where the negro children were blown up. The man who was driving the car I was in suggested that the blacks may have planted the bomb themselves to gain sympathy.

My Greek cousin Micky lives forty safe miles away from Birmingham on the banks of the Logan Martin lake system. To Micky I was always "mah crazy English cousin". On New Year's Eve I stayed with them for the first time and at midnight Micky fired six shots into the still forest. As we staggered off to bed after too much vodka Micky shouted "Hey limey?"
"What wop?"
"First one up gets busted."
"What you mean busted?"
Made the sign of a fist. "That's busted."
"Won't be me," I assured him.

There were things I tried to make him understand and he would give me a puzzled, sideways glance as we argued in the car. He was always rescuing me from some less than pleasant situation, saying: "How you bin sweet angel? Ah've been right worried about you."

It was he who said, "You know this is your home if ever you want to come here" in one of his rare serious moments. Even in our clashes over racialism he was still joking, but he noticed my narrowed stare after one of his more provocative statements: "You know this girl hates me." I may have cared for him more than anyone else in the whole venture. I think that is why I tried to get through to him. "Ah'm gonna go out and shoot me a few of them jungle-bunnies. No, but seriously Fran, ah reckon something like ten per cent of the niggers are real jewels and ah'd be proud to have 'em living in our neighbourhood. You know Miss Watts down at the restaurant, honey, she's always so neat and clean. But that other ninety per cent. Why, they're filthy honey. You seen what they've done to decent white neighbourhoods in Birmingham."

Indeed I did see, if not quite in the angle of vision they expected. Micky was to appear almost tolerant after a few days spent at Uncle Ben's. Ben had the rather macabre job of looking after a private Jewish graveyard for some of the wealthier citizens of Birmingham. They were the last whites in a now black neighbourhood. I wasn't allowed outside the confines of the cemetery into those other confines. Ben carried a loaded gun everywhere: after all, just like in 'Police Story', those damn niggers could attack at anytime. At night we drove away to their other house in a dead suburb.

The worst problem is trying to get nigger help. He can't hardly get none now they're all on welfare. The day we had a funeral in the bright sunshine Walter Chambers wrote to the bossman asking for a raise (spelt 'race'). Across the road was a rival cemetery run by a black. I could imagine the scene in Chambers' house: "What you work for them white folks fo' Walt? You kin easy get more money. They cain't manage without you." Irritated by their ingratitude, there was many a mealtime when Ben would launch a tirade over the corn bread and biscuits about the damn niggers taking "white houses, white schools and white churches and driving in their Cadillacs to collect their food stamps".

Aunt Mary confessed to being shocked that some blacks were actually travelling by plane but she allowed me to go where I pleased. Researching in West Ensley library I noticed it was story time for a group of children of mixed race. Captivated by two stories, the first about the turkey and the second about the eagle, they gobbled like turkeys and flapped their arms like eagles, each answering the other in an excited crescendo.

AFTER WASHINGTON

Though the nuns have fallen asleep
beneath the white mist wraps
as the bus slowly creeps to Pennsylvania
my eyes are still open
to a crumbling city
the startled eyes of a black worker
flagging down our bus with orange flag
for the emergency cement mixers filling
in surreptitious holes

Somewhere in the centre of the insectlights
is the one who issues confused officials.
(in the station)
"Show me your ticket"
"Hey man, what do you think I am
some kind of bum?
you sick or something?"
"I'm only doing my job"
"Why don't you search them?"

Gesture to the whites
a nun stirs uneasily in sleep
the black bible slides to her feet

SPIRALLING OUT OF MAINE

White angles razor
a fish back kicked
numbed by Ogunquit sands
'a permanent condition'
Sucked by uneven prints
the sea fragmented
our shells
splashed down
an inert brown jellyfish
or a broken lobster claw
rasping attention
at the net of an unlicensed
fisherman

In Maine
there was a clam
thrown loose to the reality
of flotsam
and now bubbles blind flesh
in its tight shell

NEWSMEN

Yes WGAL 8 newsmen
cry
They do their job
They sit in their bathtubs
think about the bloody waters
and cry
They watch governments shake
tremble over their buttered toast
and cry

We are human they assure us
even if we're not allowed
to tell you about it.

ANOTHER FAILED FUTURIST POEM

Number 964409
has tested out the John F Kennedy space center
and castigated the applied engineers
for not assembling more thunderstorms
Despite Von Braun's welcome
and the star trekked campaign of our founder
the tapes have ten years' static
Where is my five second main boost?

Now the military
plagiarise their minute men and honest johns
A skeletal staff
gloom around the space shuttle

It may carve thru the open window
to Soyuz next July
but they're having doubts about the Soviets
"They've given us a bad link up time
They're taking our ideas
Let's get back to Cape Canaveral
and quit fixing Von Braun's electric shaver"

The coaches at NASA
are for our older Greyhound drivers
Observe the museums
of previous construction space
We're all stopping
to take account
        and playback.

HEROES OF OUR TIME

THE ONE

Young men's poems
delve their sad memories into the earth
for a fecund promise
that always slides moist from their fingers

Perhaps if they took the soil itself?
and so to leaning back beneath the loam of suffocation
splaying out limbs
in hope of becoming supine clay
themselves a prostrate though muscle-bound
angel

The pictures of Caravaggio
with their creamtinted othereyed saviours
holding regular arms in commissioned framework
while beard tormented snubnosed saint Francis
collapses
on the cushioned support of his favourite boy

and do I have pity
when one whimpers for its other?

Look how it can watch and twist itself
lock and indifferently wither its sinews
be saint Jerome
use only the bone needed to carve a word
in the light of a skull

and do I
now we are one?

THE SHOOTING OF PECHORIN
for A.P.

Steady yourself at the rock edge
there, where your foot fits against the stone
and blades of complicit grass
clasp tight around your heel
you can be steady
you know it is a lie brings you here
my love, you are thinking of the wrong lie
leave it there
for now no shifts of soil
will dare dislodge beneath you
nor impact of fire push you
back
yours is the balance
because you know you know yourself

"Fixed on the wall..."

Fixed on the wall
with no apparent strings
the face of Christ
eyes averted from the light

or else he might see across the room
the Virgin Mary who croons
to a child's head
through soundless lips

On the white walls
no other adornment

Below perhaps a blanket fold
pink or purple

Two hands lock in silence
between unavoided eyes

CARNAL KNOWLEDGE

It ceased to give pleasure
the concave body which made full
became thin
Even the scooping gesture
became blunted and dull

So they held up instead
the poem above their heads
which signalled the transparence of one
for the other a moment to be gone

"This woman is reduced to a line
perhaps not even implied
What do we know of her?
Something of an intellectual bore?"

He did allow a gesture of analysis
for his seed was irretrievable
a cloud-rift of 'there might have been'
an adjunct to the morning-after kiss

"Style is excused by fever..."

Style is excused by fever
dilated beneath the eyes
of the boy whose thin veins
ran blue through your page forever

Later we know he walked away
through swung hotel doors
down imploring corridors
We know you turned your hands away
to the iron frame that became a bed
where twisted arms climb
and attendants recognise no signs
at a crossed frontier

That limpid boy
was employment for only a page
which created itself
See, it is the face of your white self

"Too blatant for deceit..."

Too blatant for deceit
you would turn your back cloth side to me
and hang its silk lining black
before my eyes
and retract all talk of the heart
for to talk of that
dare I say is also your part

In our 'communal' bath
you would lie immersed for hours
while I snatched a towel
fearing not to dry myself

"You do not think" you said
"really about death as I do
Pass me the shampoo"

PORTRAIT OF A WRITER

"He wrote for women, always for women. If he gave a poem or a story to a particular woman it was rarely the woman who had initially inspired him. Yet he always had the impression that the text belonged to her, that she had become the true owner of a certain poem or story."

In this way, his self-criticism began. A game of mirrors which created the desired effect and left me dazzled. Self-criticism, because under the pretext of writing a biography, playing the role of objective critic and quoting from an author's private unpublished diaries, he was evidently writing the story of his own life.

Most of the extracts taken from the diary concern a young girl, the writer's first love, whose Christian name we are told, but whose surname is pure fiction: 'Linda Musen'. Linda of the blond hair, cut in the nape of the neck in a style too simple not to have been expensive; Linda who wore the olive green coat; Linda, whom our author, lack of experience perhaps, failed to keep in his real life.

After watching her leave for the last time he undergoes a night of crisis, signalled in the diary by a series of metaphors which so greatly impressed the 'critic'. He points to them as evidence of the growth of an author who must rid himself of this heap of images.

These metaphors had, as their source, the name Muse, and I remember some of them: the letter M written on his forehead, M of morphine engraved on his forehead by this woman, and, at the end, he cries: 'Dreadful Muse, will I never be rid of you'.

To be faithful to the text, I should add that the critic tells us the author survived this period of despair, partly due to more successful sexual relationships. Unfairly I could add a third mirror by saying that this second stage of the author's life – that of emotional tranquillity – did not take place. Perhaps I don't have the right, but in all fairness, this portrait is only a fiction...

As a writer, then, I accuse you and will not let you be a complacent critic. This mark 'M', sign of misery and with reason! You remember the title of the film, made by that great director Fritz Lang, which was written in chalk on the murderer's back, unknown to him. It is the sign inscribed in the hollow of everyone's hand, but which our writer succeeds in planting on someone else's forehead and, simultaneously, sticking it to his own. A murderer who projects not a metaphor, this much abused word, but a symbol which shapes another, destroys another, and then the murderer feels destroyed by the reflection of his own work. This is the fundamental distinction between the metaphor and the symbol.

As I myself have assumed the role of second critic I am going to complete the history of our story 'Alfred and the Muses'. Alfred Pleasant was the pseudonym our writer chose: he wished at all costs to remain anonymous, only revealing a fragment of his game. It was indeed a competition that was at stake – a short story competition for which a small prize had been proposed. 'Alfred' won. The judge, a man of letters, himself a novelist, though little known owing to his obscure modern style, was doubtless attracted by the double game of characters. Perhaps he had even recognised a certain resemblance to his own state of mind. I suggest the possibility, I don't know for sure.

It only remains for me to mention the woman, owner for some time of the short story – one of Linda's successors. She revealed the author's name to a friend who was responsible for the competition. The letter, sending back the original manuscript to 'Alfred Pleasant' implied her knowledge of the pseudonym. The writer, laid bare, never forgave her and it was the last text she ever received from him.

Written from memory in French and translated.

4 A.M. DITCHLING RISE

– A red brick wall
teeth on edge
a finger chimney
and our bed –
"Is this *simple* enough?
my dream asked

You laughed
brown head vibrating
with the first train
on the stained pillow
Cup your hand against my forehead
A cure for The Railway's
whisky throb
our temples pulse
with the blackened viaduct
where the train winds
and my finger slides
round your eyelid

Last night the landlord wiped a glass
watched our whisky kiss, you said
"He thinks I'm doing the decent thing by you
but THE SPIRIT OF THE RAILWAY WORKER IS NOT DEAD"
chalk letters on a siding shed.

THE EZRA POUND PAPERS

There was Tom, a 'naively enthusiastic' Canadian, on his own admission. He had once met Olga Rudge when she was in Canada: she had apparently been interested in his deep blue eyes (and perhaps his logger's physique). Tom required no more than this intimation of interest. She suggested he come over and be a working guest in Marie de Rachewiltz's castle. Thus Tom was to meet not only Ezra Pound's mistress but also his daughter. A few weeks later he sent a telegram signed 'Blue Eyes' and went. At the end of his long and tortuous journey he saw, standing at the castle entrance, dressed in white gauze which seemed to float in the dim evening light, Patricia. She was the most beautiful girl he had ever seen, and the fact that she was Pound's grand-daughter only enhanced that beauty.

He was also able to meet Olga Rudge again in Venice. She rarely receives visitors. He sent a note up to her apartment saying that he would be in Chico's around the corner, if she wanted to see him. He knew that Chico's had been a favourite meeting place for Olga and Ezra. She sent a note of invitation and the first thing Tom did on entering her room was to stroke the stone head of E.P which Gaudier-Brzeska had carved and which Olga Rudge now possesses.

Tom was only one of a group of academics who came to a conference on this American poet, held at Keele University last year. There were only two 'non-professionals': one was an engineer and the other a psychiatrist who worked in Washington D.C. – someone said he looked a bit like Erlichmann, one of the Nixon gang. He was smooth, yes. Skin that was puffed and iced, small features, hair that wisped to the right. He looked at you steadily, mildly. He was not a relative collector, but when young had known the man himself. Pound was at that time an inmate of St. Elizabeth's asylum in Washington.

"I was able to talk to him then because I believed in his politics. I knew nothing about his poetry until later. He would only talk politics with his visitors, you know. Only once did I, personally, see him get angry with a visitor. It was when a woman brought her Jewish friend without first asking. He didn't tell her to get out, exactly, but…

Ezra used to take his women visitors behind the bushes, you know… He was an immensely strong man then. I played tennis with him, too." The psychiatrist made a sweeping gesture with his arm to imitate the strength of the literary lion. "He declined so quickly after he left. You've seen the pictures of him. He suddenly became an old man."

"There were those," I said, "who thought it would have been better for him to stay there."

"Oh. I don't know. He so much wanted to leave…"

"Yes. I know; but when he did leave he collapsed into senility. Perhaps it was a little like the London years. He needed people around him in order to produce his best work, even those he hated most."

"Yes, he was surrounded by people. You may be right." He suddenly laughed and became excited. "But he dropped us all after he left. Even C. who had spent three years in jail for him. Three years in jail. He just came out and told C. that he couldn't see him anymore. He had been told to drop his connection with C. if he wanted to get out. So he did."

The man who said perhaps the most to me was another Canadian. Each time I saw him I found it impossible to remember the physical details of his appearance, yet his words, about the lecture he was going to deliver stayed in my mind. At first I had not understood him. I said, referring to the imminent lecture: "You can get it published, I suppose."

"No. Charlie Terrell will think it too critical." Charlie Terrell is the editor of the official Pound magazine.

"Of Pound, you mean."

"Yes."
"Oh."

Now the lines concentrated towards him. The room was
dark. The rain riveted down upon the Midlands, the flat lands,
the home lands. Terrell was chairman then, upright in his chair,
arms folded, the stiff unhappy general of an army about to be
defeated. Briefly his army of contributors would be swept aside
by the spectres one man raised.

EP SPEECH AGAINST THE PROCESS

Between the morning and the afternoon
between the bright wooden slats of the room
which cradled the caught sounds
of the Provençal lyric
and the dark ceiling timber
which ran towards another speaker
his voice confusing with the rain:

> "This was the man who used a swastika in his letterhead
> who praised his hostess for
> the Aryan character of her guests
> who took Mussolini's weakest jest
> as the greatest sign of intelligence
> If a blind error was committed under Hitler's direction
> it could only occur because he was 'furious from perception'
> who believed like the Führer
> that 'Humanity is malleable mud'"

Ignore the chips from the stone
Any sculptor would

THE RIGHT BALANCE

LE JUSTE MILIEU

1

If you want silence
if you want a poem
breaking beyond the page
we must not take each others' traces
breaking the ice in the mud
avoiding the brown frost of the lake
for all that the snow can give you
    you already have
a photograph

II

Saint George and the dragon
defunct saint at Bâle cathedral
turns a spear through mouth and tail
You have the photograph now
do not develop it
kneel squint against the sun
for some other red statue
(woman with a lampshade
wearing a carpet)
leave negative the head
in the cold
in the turn of a collar

III

Although rigidity was the accusation
when a thrust of the hand could not make the knee
bend
away from the refusing body
Touch your hips now
Can they yet move or turn?
Look strangely at the hand placed there
From your head it is a stranger's hand

IV

She had known him for a short time. He was French, she was English.

"I would never have thought," she said to him one evening, as they returned from a bistro "that I could speak in French to someone like this."
"Oh yes, it's possible" he assured her and his car travelled quickly through the night. "We must always talk to each other" he said "there must never be a lack of equality, an unequal balance."

He talked to her about the right balance. "It is possible to create 'un juste milieu'." It would exist for them. He taught her to ski and each time she fell he asked:
"Can you manage?" ("Tu t'en sors?")
Afterwards he said "You did well for a beginner".
"Yes. I need about half an hour to get used to it and then I feel all right…"
"It's a question of finding the right balance."

One night she said to him: "You know I have thought of a fine short story in the style of Henry James. There would be a girl, an English girl who meets a Frenchman and who believes him when he talks of the 'juste milieu' which exists between them. She constructs her whole life around that phrase and it has all the significance of a true religion for her. From it emanates subtle, valued connotations which she sustains with all the imagination and sensitivity of which she is capable. And you know all Jamesian heroines are capable of an inexhaustible appreciation. Until one day she hears the young French man use this phrase casually to explain a skiing technique. She suddenly understands, a blinding revelation, that the beautiful phrase was only a cliché."
He smiled "No, it wasn't altogether a cliché."

NORTH FACE

for Gerard

If the Alps are grey-shouldered
where are their faces?

Shrunken faces
tight line against the pillow
call it: 'tête reduite'

A slope you can never climb
though you hack one line above another

'But you are blue with fear!' he said

At night the white wax drips
Who has not woken in the early hours
and seen the face of a stranger shining
absorbed in the linen?

When I woke I saw my glasses
upended in the snow beyond my head
and it was not the mountain which bent
to hand them back

FROM THE JURA

Vertical climb of the funiculaire
reading what do I know? philosophy
Cab climbs above the snow line
halfway the rails part
as the two cabs pass
the drivers jump across
one always stays below
the other at Chaumont funi station

Following blue ribbons tied to branches
left for cross country skiers
the ski tracks
my boot marks
on the path between the dark pines
come into a field
low stone wall
on the horizon the 'three chimneys'
Eiger Mönch Jungfrau
below us the flat cantonal fog

Is this the path back?
I run across the field
stop a tractor driver
– Where is Chaumont?
– This is Chaumont
– Yes, but where is the funi?

THE CONTEMPORARY POET IN PARIS
for Yves Bonnefoy

As I unfolded my Michelin Montmartre
it was raining
and street numbers slid me down
the steep cobbles of Rue Lepic
stopped only by an excavator
whose concrete bones lay in square clay holes
I read in *The Times*
that mediaeval gypsum mines
have left the poets' hill a hollow
to be collapsed by new construction.

At the bottom of the slope I found your postwar
apartment and from a baker's shop
I watched its hard grey façade,
wondered which round window was yours
At the entrance a microphone informed me
'M. Bonnefoy is out of the country.'

THE ATTRACTION OF AMERICAN EXPRESS

Sussex graduates, female of course, took temporary jobs there and told us of its sunless atmosphere. It did not deter them entirely since, if you're female and a graduate with some secretarial qualifications, it was still better than the dole. All the windows at American Express are curtained and the exterior world cannot penetrate. It stands like a stranded time capsule; a piece of the futurist, profitable American dream which has broken off from the mother ship and landed on the Victorian terraces of Brighton. Its tiered design prompted one bright young man to compare it to a wedding cake: all the walls are white icing and all the curtained windows are blue. With some idea of integration, or domination, they painted the backs of a nearby row of terraces white; with the permission of the owners I think.

It was just the moment for a local television reporter to stand, ankle deep in office floor carpet and gesture to the entirely wasted areas of corridor space, in yet another newly built, central Brighton, office complex, in contrast to the thousands who were either homeless or living in substandard council estates on the outskirts of town. Slums like Moulsecoomb. I looked up from Utopian visions and heard the new sermon: American Express shall inherit the earth.

American Express was in our area: Kemptown. I belonged to a local community action group which was largely inspired by a husband and wife team, both of whom were history lecturers at Sussex University. They bore no resemblance to the characters in Malcolm Bradbury's *The History Man*, although they were greatly involved in putting their socialist principles into practice. They tried to be as self-effacing as possible but everyone knew that they were the ones who could obtain the necessary grant for a community project and, above all, could defy authorities. American Express was trying to find a leisure centre for its staff. The eventual site of this leisure centre was arousing some anxiety amongst concerned Kemptown residents as rumours circulated that it might even be one of the schools that Brighton Council (Tory) was hoping to close down. As it happened our particular sector of Kemptown was looking for its own social centre to replace one we had lost, due to local disorganization and the council seizing its chance. Our socialist leader was a realist and did not avoid painless compromise: a deputation was sent to American Express confronting them with the rumour that they were trying to buy up local schools. The public relations sector became extremely agitated and sought to conciliate the residents. A tentative agreement was reached on the possibility of a shared leisure centre which would be entirely financed by American Express.

I moved to another area and American Express merged into the urban hillside. I tried to write about Utopian images again, and several months later I travelled to Paris with the intention of meeting the author of one alternative vision.

I didn't meet him – he was away on a lecture tour in America – but I did meet Danielle, who told me her life story on the boat crossing from New Haven to Dieppe. I wouldn't normally have chosen her as a travelling companion but it was a quiet time of the year. She wore bright, sleek clothes and her hair was carefully blond. Her story had all the indiscreet charm of the bourgeoisie, set in the vacations when her husband tried to be unfaithful and she herself began an affair with a married Englishman, bored by the demands of his wife and children. "I did not like him at all when I first met him. He was very cold, very English and I thought that he treated his wife badly. But then I got to know him better and I realised that it was not all his fault – his wife was also to blame."

The Englishman's name was Colin, which, as Danielle remarked is also the name of a fish in French. She had cards, modest tokens of unlimited spending power, which bore his name and his status: Director of American Express. Danielle had decided to give up her job in Paris and go and live with Colin in Brighton, but she was already afraid of growing too dependent on him. She had taught Colin French but he was too impatient to teach her English, and Colin's parents still preferred his first wife. Danielle sought a friend in Brighton and hoped that I might be one. She insisted on taking me out for a meal in Paris and I felt clumsy and shabby next to her practised radiance. The better if not the best restaurants knew her and she knew them: they created a mutually responsive effect. Yet even this world was innocent, I believed, compared to Colin's.

During our evening out the car broke down and while five Parisian policemen and Danielle tried to mend it I took care of her bracelet. The next day it was still in my handbag and I had to return to Danielle's apartment. I found her throwing clothes in a suitcase, in a rush to fetch Colin from the Paris branch of American Express and drive him to the airport. We were late, Danielle was tearful and Colin lectured her furiously on the loss of dignity she had caused him. I disliked him immediately. His French was surprisingly good. He looked at me through the car mirror and we both knew that Danielle had chosen the wrong person.

I did see Danielle once after she had moved to Brighton. She told me that she and Colin were arguing too much. He was intensely anxious about his work and believed that his new boss took less interest in his opinions. Some of his frustration he directed at her and one night she had cried. He thought she cried because he hurt her, but really she cried because she was afraid she didn't love him any more.

I told her a little about my life: my family background and the frustration I experienced in my work.

"You know, you're just like Colin," she said.

46

GERMANY IN AUTUMN

ANNIVERSARY POEM

Came into your country
Four sick faces stared from the customs booth
TERRORISTEN !
Fair uniformed young man took unsmiling my passport,
saw my treason
What use these blown up faces?
(A quoi bon? in French)
Not to help an arrest
but to define the line the patriot treads

In the morning your face blurs
in my eyes, the coarse outline of your head

    Anna didn't like the content of this poem. When I
explained to her that this was the anniversary of World War
Two, a fact that she, a German was unaware of, although
English t.v. had been running historic newsreels in celebration
of the event, she insisted that the analogy was entirely false.
She is politically leftwing but firmly opposed to the Baader-
Meinhof group. Perhaps she disliked the content because it was
a celebration of another anniversary: that of my first meeting
with the "bear". She found him selfish and calculating. At the
time she came to stay he was more interested in Georg Lukács
than anyone else. She also knew that he was my main reason
for coming to Germany.

    When I arrived at Anna's house her family were all
gathered and talking about her love for her East German cousin
Peter.
    "To me," said her father, "it is like a love affair during the
war. A girl writes to a young soldier in the trenches and it is all
very romantic as long as they remain at a distance."
    "How do you know if you will get on together?" asked her
sister.

"Will he be able to find a job here or will he be dependent on you?" asked her mother

"But really Anna, ten thousand pounds for his release! Can't you find a cheaper man somewhere else?" asked her father.

"You don't have to marry do you?" asked grandmother. "You could just live together at first." She seemed to be satisfied by the idea that a marriage did not have to take place.

Even with my limited knowledge of German I could follow most of their arguments and I had to add "you've never lived with anyone before, Anna."

Peter had married and divorced and Anna said that both of them had tried to forget the existence of the other. Her forgetting had only included brief affairs. I had to admire her romantic desire for unity.

When all the relatives had left I looked around her new place. All her belongings were in a more perfect order. Ordnung. Files, books, tapes, photographs … her large preparation desk, each drawer labelled with the appropriate class number – the class she was teaching at school. I lounged on the sofa, refused most of the food that was offered, and in the days which followed read her beloved Kerouac or went for solitary walks during her teaching hours.

Hundertwasser prints were in the bedroom and perhaps they inspired her to sit up in her sleep at dawn and say "The windows are covered with lollipops." She got up at six a.m. to begin preparation but we sometimes argued after midnight.

"What is your thesis about?" she asked

"Oh I don't know … Surrealism, Abstract Expressionism." I named a few poets and painters including Jackson Pollock.

"I know his work" she said, "he does those things a child of five could do. I've got some reproductions. I'm sure I have." She got out of bed at two a.m. to go and look for them. "What is the value of this?" waving a colour supplement at me. "I could do better."

"It was an expression of inward desires and motivation. An attempt to free them."

"But what use was any of it? Of what importance to anyone else in society?"

"They were committed to social change, they…" I had my doubts too, but she was redirecting my attitudes.

In the morning, drinking something she had provided to improve my health and still arguing…

"It takes five minutes to produce something like that. Where is the skill, the artistry?"

"You're so bourgeois," I exploded and hated myself. I'd vowed never to use that word. She smiled triumphantly and with a deep sense of loss.

AUTUMN NOW
for Anna

I recited Rilke to you or tried to,
as we climbed the path through the vineyard:
the slopes above industrial Esslingen,
where the Gastarbeiter lent on their hoes,
conversed in the sun in another language,
watched us climb
"Twenty per cent of the population is Greek or Turkish"
"Herr es ist Zeit" I persisted,
seeking the climax of a figure disappearing,
erratic molecules combining with the wet descending leaves,
the path awash,
in a rain that won't leave him

And the same night your friends knew the poem and they were
political activists. Ro was also a writer and a judge of other
people's writing. "So much of what is sent me is so subjective.
so personal." I sympathised. Ro's husband came in. He was a
socialist politician in local government.

Anna said "You can look for the Rilke here. I'm sure Ro
has a copy."

"What was that?" the husband asked. I began to quote
"Herr, es ist Zeit" and he finished for me. We found the
poem and Ro said "I used to like Rilke very much. You have
to admire what he does with the German language. It's really
wonderful." She recited a few lines. "But I rejected his ideas
when I was sixteen," and she closed the book.

We talked about the lives of artists. She had recently been
reading the journals of Thomas Mann. "That is such a dreadful
image of the artist" she said "with his precisely ordered,
insulated existence" and she gave examples of Mann's daily
routine.

Finally I said "My ideal of the artist is not entirely socially responsible. It is of someone like Kerouac, someone living on the edge of society, but who is not shut away from it in a tidy study. Someone who is poor, who travels and observes. Even Rilke, at least when he lived in a crumbling Parisian hotel room, cannot be entirely condemned."

certain things could be forgiven, accepted,
even the vision of autumn,
"when leaves downrain"

LETTERS TO HEIDELBERG

When I showed Andreas the 'Anniversary poem' he asked whether I could not perhaps link his name with a patriotic theme instead and, laughing, he added: "I understand poetic licence, but I have to think of my future."

In Heidelberg he was the student prince. His room on the Hauptstrasse was small and bare, but we chose imitation velvet curtains and the colour of the walls was fine. Hauptstrasse now, ringing, jingling bells, the pony cart is fussing past, view of C & A, neat divisions in flag colours, divisions in sweet colours, peaks on red plastic caps. If you look out the back you see flat shadows, landlords saving on expense, saving the family: they do not need to advertise. The Biedermeier portrait of the writer in his garret, huddled in bed, fully clothed, studying, with an umbrella above him to catch the drips from the leaking roof. The modern version of this reads: "'Only poverty produces greatness.' A general truth. Authors demand royalties."

The student prince will show you round the town: "This is where the student prince used to live. It was very squalid. This is where the flood water from the river Neckar came to in 1977 and the student prince had to swim across the street to get his provisions." In the museum you can see portraits of the other student princes, exotically dressed and reclining on silk couches, smoking a pipe perhaps, sword propped against the couch. Perhaps they still live in the fraternity houses exclusively situated on the hillside just where the woods begin.

Today's student prince also knows how to use weapons. He was a soldier.
"What did you do in the army, baby?"
"I resigned once. Or at least I wrote a letter of resignation and left it in the desk drawer where unfortunately the sergeant found it. I was confined to office duties for a week – the worst

punishment. I got a certain physical satisfaction out of digging holes for drains, muscular exhaustion. And," he smiled, "a satisfaction out of the sound that my army boots made when we marched on parade. I was excited then. I was part of something larger than myself. You can't deny it, you can't."

In another modern version there is a photograph of an S.S. gathering in Heidelberg castle during the war, and all the eyes have been carefully masked as if to say that they are alive and well, perhaps in Heidelberg itself and would prefer anonymity.

We sang the folksongs of 1848. They were good songs, written by men fleeing from despotic rulers, rallying the people, all the people with their words, and all the people singing – "Alte wie die Junge" – to do something: "Tun wir etwas dazu." Whether you hammer nails into shoes, or bear a cross, you can help to make one Germany. And so came "Deutschland über alles", itself a product of this enlightened, heroic period. Not a song of domination but of unification. Now we have the songs of Wolf Biermann.

But we never sang Biermann's political songs, only the one which tells of breakfast with Tina. He beat out the rhythm with an egg spoon and then with his feet, bouncing me until the bouncy, laughing rhythm slows into a deep, wordless sexual pause, and then starts again. We ate all the typically German dishes, which he cooked and he would push food into my mouth with his tongue.

In bed he could be an Alsatian dog, pawing me, licking me in a friendly manner, then suddenly barking and snapping ferociously, so that I covered my head and laughed and screamed at him to stop. "Alsatians," he explained, "are often taught to go for the arm of an intruder and not to let go, so if you protect your arm the Alsatian will harmlessly sink his fangs into the protective covering while you drag it round the house looking for something to smash on its head."

"You are someone who is in love with the bear and afraid of him," he said.

In Heidelberg he was Dr. Faustus. He always made someone less confident than himself play God, and snarled out the lines of Faustus' speech:
"Heisse Magister, heisse Doktor gar" ('I am called Master, I am called Doctor'), with all the contempt of an old style actor. He was an intellectual who wrote: "We Germans when we suffer from Weltschmerz must either cry or build systems."

Sometimes he built systems and everything and everyone else ceased to matter. Even the taste of chocolate cake became less important.

We climbed to the Philosophenweg, there you will find the stone inscribed with Hölderlin's famous lines, although there are more popular odes to the city.

"Lange lieb' dich schon, möchte dich, mir zur Lust,
Mutter nennen, und dir schenken ein kunstlos Lied"

1

Where your velvet curtains are
and the green walls rest your mind

there the low mattress
lies easy on the floor

Where the few shelves are
an old pair of plimsolls

Where no hearing is
except your body

Where the door is closed and open and

"People commit suicide here too"

you told me

I know

2

In the castle
speak softly
softer than the tourists

Pause in the green glare
which plays on Goethe's exploded tower

Cast your eyes towards the cascade
steps I sat on

Do not forget Neptune
If someone fell from a turret
do not laugh too long

This song was something by Wagner
which you did not recognise
let me hum louder

3

I would have called you mother
or father in this case
but now the leaves are lifted up
and I look up into their thin stirring stomachs
reach for green paint on a roller
soaking the leaf onto the page
as we did at the end of every Nature Walk
except the one which goes through the "Philosophers' Way"

Do you go there alone
Do you see the bum who shuffles
to a cleft in the forest where the water comes down?

LOVE POEM

"Cupid comes with black hair and a moustache"
(Dylan)
The hooks of your charred beard
fall from the yellow skin wax,
thin nostrils ridge your face
you are on hunger strike again
a child who makes a statement
then runs from the family meal
your eyes threaten from the darkest
tunnel wall a wooden train
But when your lips thicken
the creature slips out
and tastes the world,
are caught in my flesh

FREE UNION

With your hair of wire borrowed from no-man's land
of a forest at the onset of night
of a fakir's bed

with your nose of a cliff ridge
Striding Edge shaking off walkers

with your beard of burnt paper
ever curling away from its own expansion
with your beard that threatens your mouth of cherry liqueur
your mouth of dye water from a Grantham factory

with your back of a bus
moving out into city traffic

with your spine of perfectly spaced steps

with your waist of a beech tree
of a concrete column
of a letter box
of a profaned object
made of cold metal
made of ridged bark

leaning and upright
above the snow floor
above the concrete slabs

with your thoughts at telescopic range

with your fingers of gelignite
with your flannel fingers
in a static blanket

with your fingers of hooks
to suspend their own questions

with your balls of rag dolls
taking in the demand
of every child's hand
with your ripe gooseberry balls
inside a cluster of thorns

with your penis of an old maid
raised by salvation's kiss
the most grateful face I know
with your penis of rock candy
ready to be broken
by the first careless holidaymaker
with your coach tour wheel penis
ready to impress with tarmac facts
your penis a potholer's torch
finding the rock divide

with your eyes
lying at the bottom of a button tin
with your eyes of discarded pebbles
with your eyes
of an unforgiving projector reel
and the dust revolving in its shaft of light

After André Breton's 'L'Union Libre'. A surrealist idea reversed.

THE COMMUNITY PROJECT

THE COMMUNITY PROJECT

The lower hills are the ones they used
For Sale tacked hugely on the Rochdale mill
My people are a people learning the difference
between detergents and I teach them to use fly killer
See hand, see spray
Their children play in the gutter water smiling
There is no war and the council has constructed metal
elephants for you

He stopped the car just off the motorway, somewhere in the
          Pennines
and we followed the sheep track with no way down to the river
Looking across the hills his arm bent around me
He said "Shall we go on?" I said no.

HIGHGATE CEMETERY

Victorian melodrama is a specialized pleasure
puckering out our smocks in trout fishing days
parsimony hugs the outer lip which is still full
and speaks a perfect message
but the chain now moves from one cog
to the next even forgetting the oil
men conspire to fix brackets on rusty
cemetery gates and
this is the only way I can see rust now.

He notices the 'revolutionary party of Brent
secondary school' and that the Chilean Marxists can't spell.
I notice that the Bangladeshi Marxists
have left their bouquet in its plastic wrapper,
exhalations obscure flowers. Poor Jenny.
No not read never read
Indoctrinated by Edmund Wilson instead.

Sisters of Bethany, three names to each small
metal plaque on a metal stick, a cheap alloy and
I once marked hidden treasure with wooden sticks in
the sand at the vicarage garden fête,
but the Sisters pursue a scorched earth policy, huddled
and bent above the brown grass.

Mary Ann Cross
the cause of Mary Ann hidden
from the main path
This trinity of Mary Ann, George and
the one she called daughter.
No heads, one epigraph.
(Only the daughter talks and talks
dream on Revlon)
But she is dry eyed after the thunderstorm,
after the flood. It is time to visit the doctor's wife.

DECONSTRUCTION

I saw you emerge as a rat
in white plaster dust shining
your eyes and nose up towards me

I saw you chew over the joists
suck out the juice from the backbones
and leave a small pile of twigs on the table
which I cleared away

Behind the skirting board you found
a mummified rat
spreadeagled in dessication
only a wind dried duck in the window
of a Chinese restaurant
but grey as a crevice

Later it dangled in the car window
"How could you" I said
as we passed Kew Gardens
"My aunt used to take me to the Chinese pavilion"
you replied
"I asked her why all the steps were broken
and she said that my uncle had done it"

When we came back Rentokil stood
on the doorstep.

It was a warm sunny morning in April.

SARI

I am standing in a chiffon sari
She put me in her petticoat and
her sister's blouse because
I am bigger than her
Then she took the cloth stretched
it out and I held the outstretched cloth
She wrapped it around me making
the three folds or
if you want it tighter make it five
'Tighter it is better for work'
Because the chiffon is all borders
you can refind the pattern
however you fold it
'If you want to be Moslem put
it over your head' and she did
'No, no I do not want to be Moslem'
'Alright.' she said.

You move slowly when you see the straight lines
in the mirror

In the living room
the men
are solving the new maths

WEAR YOUR POPPY WITH PRIDE

It was the first weekend in October 1982. I was thinking of the pleasure of spending a weekend in Norwich, where I used to be a student. I slung my bike into the guard's van of the weekend train. The train was completely full and several people sat in the guard's van. I sat next to someone from a parachute regiment.

He was blond, goodlooking, the Aryan type. I was almost seduced by the gold necklace he wore. It was delicately crafted gold, similar to my mother's necklace but longer. He would talk more than me, although we would have come to silence. That day he had been to a memorial service for the men in his regiment who died in the Falklands.

"I'm getting out of the army when my time is up this year. Try and get into the fire brigade like my dad. Think I stand quite a good chance. Running over mountains with your pack on and living in holes is not my idea of fun.

"I have travelled a lot with the army. Seen some interesting places."

"Were you able to get out; wasn't it difficult?" I thought of barracks.

"I got out when I was on leave. Not all the chaps did. Some just stayed in and got drunk all the time. Not me." For a while he talked about Berlin, and the East Germans he had met. Then he said:

"The Falklands war was futile. It was as if one of the smaller Channel Islands belonged to Argentina and they never did anything to it for a hundred years or more. We moved a few soldiers onto it, and they sail across the Atlantic to claim it back."

"Is there anything there?"

"No, nothing.

"When we got to Goose Green the Argentinians weren't expecting us. The first Argentinian we saw, a youngster, stood there with his mouth open. We shouted at him to raise his hands. He didn't know any English of course, so he just stood, arms at his sides. We riddled him with bullets and moved on. Later though, it was us or them, bullets whistling round our heads. The bullets can do terrible things. They can travel up a man's body, from his leg to his head." He mimicked its action. "These high velocity bullets go into the body making a very small hole, but they suck everything into it."

The train was rattling and I had difficulty hearing his words, but saw his gestures.

"The bullet comes out of the body, out of a man's back, with a hole the size of two fists."

He put his fists together

"The Argentinian bodies were terribly multilated. Some were just torsos.

"What Colonel Jones did was unnecessary, suicidal. The Argentinians were going to surrender anyway."

"Rather like the Crimea" I said.

"Not quite.

"I shot down some Argentinian helicopters. Notches on my gun."

"What?"

"The score on my gun."

Some black youths stumbled drunk into the guards' van. The middle-class whites moved to make room for them, smiling in a friendly manner. The guards glared. My soldier scarcely flickered a recognition of their presence. But he had to talk to me, the information officer.

"Never did any work at school. Just moved around with my mates. Went straight into the army.

"I want to do more halo parachuting. That's what the SAS do. You go up to 25 or 35,000 feet. It's free fall to start with.

That's a great sensation. It's as if there's an enormous hand holding you up, as you fall slowly."

"But it doesn't prevent you from falling?"

"No." He smiled. "The other day I pulled the ripcord and my parachute didn't open, but it was only caught in a vacuum. For a moment I thought I'd had it."

"Did you see your whole life pass in front of you?"

"Yes, and it was going that way." His hand pointed rapidly across his body.

ORGREAVE

"They're running through a corn field
and now through a field of barley"

The miners from the police

Such precision
from our war correspondent!

The precision of journalism which adds
nothing to the story

They are not running from the police
They are running from the precise outline of a black
slag heap or a black mill
above the village rubbish tip
next to the Esso garage

seen through the corn field
(and they were all corn fields)
seen through the poppies
seen through the sunset
seen though the white sticks marking out
the site of the next council estate.

GREEKS

On Fonthill Road
male eyes watch to see
if I have a pattern or
am interested in their patterns
Angela Chic
Angel trimmings
Sometimes half seen
are the sewing women
The history of the seamstress survives

One more shirt before dawn

Greek Cypriot that is
Koulla, who married Wayne, our New Zealander
"Koulla. Is that what they call them in New Zealand"
sd Paul who thought it was Kiwi for Sheila
We were glad he didn't take up with an Asian girl
though Koulla's dad made threats
"Why?" asked Wayne
"Because I'm poor bloody Greek that's why."
It took them months to make the sugar roses on the wedding cake
each petal shaped by hand

And I sd "Go downstairs and iron your shirt.
Go on"
"What if I meet someone on the stairs" you sd
"I know. I'll talk about the influence of Greek poetry on the
early Pound"

BRITISH MUSEUM

"They always get things wrong
on the exhibition labels"
he said, looking like someone from a housing co-op
We were looking at a gittern
"It can't have been played with a plectrum" he said
"No it can't" you calmly agreed
"But it does say that it was later adapted
to be played as a violin."

I met Chris in a quilted anorak trying
to keep warm amongst the Assyrians.

We had money for the Anglo-Saxon art exhibition
for the gold crosses and brooches

"The cross says: I am drenched and bloody"
They speak to us in runes
"Arthur ordered me to be made"
Tongues of fire glowing out of the manuscript
In the reign of King Cnut

"I think it's a scheme drawn up by Canute to
make the water flow uphill. Lincoln, the worst managed
city in England." Uncle Tom writing from Station Farm.
"We've had a good corn year but the potatoes have no life
in them a good crop ½ out ½ in but we shall survive that's
more than many Ethiopians will."

And they were much preoccupied with Doomsday.

THE DAMP PATCH

We had a very interesting damp patch today. Or rather it was not the damp patch which was interesting but the people around it. This morning I had just finished tidying up and listening to Ian Dury talking about the glamour of wafting through life, when Phil, our architect, arrived with a dampometer. He'd grown a beard and I wasn't sure that it suited him. There was something more untidy about him than usual and he seemed in a hurry.

"I thought Ann Taylor, the development worker, was coming too."

"I did ring her, but she said she would rather not be involved unless it was really necessary."

I offered him tea, and at first he accepted, but later left without mentioning it again. He measured the damp in the stained and bulging magnolia paintwork, and there was obviously a problem. "The wall is damp, but I'm not sure what's causing it. It could still be water trapped in the wall, which is penetrating through. In which case I'll get the builders to put on waterproof sand cement render."

"You mean that isn't what they're using already?" I was only half listening, still thinking that this would go away, or be taken care of.

"The builders are very anxious to finish and get their money. I'll instruct them to come in on Tuesday and hack off this plaster. Have you got a crayon?"

"But it might not be water trapped in the wall?"

"No, but I can't see where else it could be coming from."

Later in the morning he rang me again. "I've been asking advice, and it's possible that the dampness might be caused by the cold bridging."

"Could be, but I have no idea what you're talking about."

"Sorry, these jargon words. I mean there's concrete under the sill, which is cold and may cause condensation."

"Is that the builders' fault?"

"No, it's mine. It might be possible to put a thin layer of wood on the wall, or polystyrene. I must talk to your flatmate Janet and find out what would be aesthetically acceptable to her." He was boggling my mind, to quote Joseph Heller. We discussed Janet's phone number and said goodbye.

I was half asleep after lunch when the phone rang. It was Janet who expanded on Phil's alternatives, and her own rising anxieties.

"A layer of wood. What on earth would it look like? I don't feel I can agree to anything. I would have done if he'd sounded confident, but he seems so unsure." I began to think.

"It isn't your decision or mine. Tell Phil that I'm going to get a second opinion, now, and I'll ring him back."

So I biked over to Colin's to get some technical suggestions. Colin was out so I left a message. Then I went to the co-op secretary for advice, but still no reply, so I decided to go straight to the development worker, who I had never met before. When I arrived at her office it was locked. It was now mid afternoon. But soon a small, merry group returned from a leaving party. Ann Taylor was one of them. At first I thought I couldn't get her attention, but as I explained the story, she concentrated and responded. "Phil told me there was only one outstanding problem, but he didn't tell me that it was this. Did he tell you the damp reading?"

"No, and if he had it wouldn't have meant anything."

"I suppose this is really the development worker's job."

"Yes," agreed another woman who had just resigned. Ann rang Phil and spoke to him, while smiling at me, both of us aware of his discomfort. Phil must have confused me so much, I reasoned, *because* he wanted to force me to make him behave correctly. But maybe I'm getting Jamesian here.

"Whatever you do" said Ann "don't let him give the builders any money. None of the retention money until this is sorted out." The other woman was even surer of this, and the three of us were perfectly clear. So when I see Phil I know what to say. I have been instructed. Anyway Colin has been round.

"It's soaking wet," he said. "In fact I can smell rot. Oh, dear I have absolutely no idea what's causing it."

USCITA

We had to leave Venice
because there were no hotels that year
though *Stern* says that there is a new lunatic asylum

Sweets in the streets
but all the signs were completo
Can't take a hotel out of the station
so take a train out the other way
Uscita.

Who are these Italians who want you to get
lost
Uscita.

You came upon me in the train so quickly
Italian stallion saying
– Love. We make love. Amore.
    It is terrible I must go for soldier
– You are young, I say,
    You are twenty and I am thirty
Your fingers search along the base of mine
and do not find the Signora
I say – Say dove. How do you say dove?
Dove long open O
Dove sta memoria, donatello
I say – Your hair is like wire
– Yes, yes, the barbers make it so
Up and up they make it go
My hand bounces off
I say – You are made for love
But I feel your lips like rubber and
my tongue works against yours which works
so hard.

EIGHT DEAD AS GANG FIRES
ON NAPLES CROWD

On the streets of Naples
they will sell you paper tissues
fazoletti
and in the cafés
while you eat tagliatelli
or on the bus where
the English woman who married
an Italian said
"My husband is a qualified lawyer but
he can't practice.
You can't be an honest man
and practise law here"
And George said
"Look at those buildings"
"The garden sheds?"
"People live there since the earthquake.
Look at the apartments. Those concrete spans
weren't made to last"
Torn concrete tissues

On the streets of Pompeii
we shared bread rolls called
rosetti
We tore them between our fingers
and wrapped them in tissue.

RECONSTRUCTION

Black Périgord
Black Virgin at Rocamadour Roc
    ama
    dour
Blue black curved petal
dragonfly clings to the leaf
Black ants in the coarse grass
The only face she saw that day
was in the uprooted tree

Time to shit and move on
She covered her shit with dead leaves
and a stone
A moment of joy
like the opening scene of Wim Wenders' film
Im Lauf der Zeit
In the run of time
So much better than *Paris-Texas*

Try Chicago-Périgord
And Franklin Collery-Combs
The G.I.'s bastard son who
lost the United States as soon as he was born
I am here to tell you how
ephemeral they are
but also to shake you from all traditions
except your own

"We are now in Mas David, and I work very much on this
formidable stone house, and that terrific garden. I was houseman,
I am slave, or house-slave. But a happy one!"

THE SEX OF ART

NIKI ST. PHALLE

or 'The entrance of the only woman in the breast of the group'
(1960 The New Realists)

Saint Sebastian or Portrait of my lover
Shirt with nails banged in
Head dart board, with darts thrown in
Empowering

If you do that
If you knock the nails in
If you shoot the rifle
If you hold the rifle, butt hard against your shoulder
If you shoot the plaster
If the worst meal you ever cooked pours out
Pow pow pow

Saint Sebastian
Is it you too?
It's the menstrual flow
Flou
Femme éclatée

He was a stuffed shirt
'I never shot God only the church'
Christ you pointed the gun at him
and helped Sebastian to die all over again
and properly this time

TINGUELY

Now
the henpecked machine stutters
its hooks grasp
spasmodically
He explains the deterioration
of its movement

Little girls in velvet
hesitate press
a foot on the button
look up with dislike at my
dislike
I watch the cycling machine which operates
a mad pram and a nail which scratches
a circle in a metal plate
It is difficult for a child to reach the pedals
The boys seek the greatest speed which
the machine diffuses
I love the boy who holds himself on the pedals
more off than on the seat or
the one who clutches the tattered book for extra
leverage
The little girls are in skirts or their heels slide
off the pedals

GWEN JOHN

On Sunday I relax with Melissa
I sit on the planks of a corner seat in the garden
She is stripping a chair she found in the street
She's sitting on the grass
chair firmly grasped
her back to me
her bare legs spread out
one foot flexed with dark red painted toenails
her skirt with its big red rose pattern spreading
on the grass
her pink sweatshirt, and her long dark hair partly
pulled across by a clip
She scrapes and scrapes away
at the paint
The chair is patchy shades of brown
the brown which approaches and recedes
in numbered tones
"I haven't got the patience for that" says Mary picking
green beans for our supper

Three quarter length young women and girls
by Gwen John
I liked the noses most of all
You don't get the noses and the nostrils in men's
paintings of women
What a relief to see the real self staring at you
but so remote that you can't reach her
gathered in, collected

THE DINNER PARTY

Vulva
"Vagina, vagina! What kind of word is that?" he said
I can say cunt
but I wouldn't to you

Vulva
A creature she said, pulsating, creating
pushing off the plate with every muscle

I was disappointed, yes
Perhaps he was right

This effort can only exist within a limited format –
the plate – she explained

He paused by Emily Dickinson's plate
amazed by all the frills

"And that white sustenance – despair"
        and that white
sustenance
        despair
and that white sustenance
sus
        ten
        ance
And that White Sustenance
Despair –

In the folds of the vulva
"You're very labial"

M stands for the millennium
(It used to stand for your Metaphor and Muse
Symbolic Murder)

In white work
White silk thread on white
    satin
I was spiralling out of Maine
White angles razor

The second time
I took the Judy Chicago tape and
she put the earpiece over my ear
"There's a piece of your hair caught"
And at the end another attendant was laughing 'hysterically'
"It's because we've been working here for eleven hours."

HOLLAND : ITHACA

HOLLAND : ITHACA

One clear morning she knew
that blue sea was hers
was with her beyond the porthole
Although
she walks with the youngest daughter
of the queen, who
suffers, who is retarded
You can see it in the way she walks
on the ship's deck bending
her head

This is our port
This is Den Haag
Not a picture porthole
not a lifebuoy
on a packet of Capstan cigarettes
Here in the breakfast lounge
we eat slowly
Others are falling over suitcases to the
gangway
Someone will meet us
We could stay here all morning

The bay of Dexia and the mountain are one
To you it was just another porthole
'I think you must be Odysseus…'

On deck the princess walks
She will change her name
and marry an American
I seem to remember

ITHACA : THE HAVEN

Suddenly an explosion
an earthquake?
I don't want to register earthquakes
Meanwhile the Lord of the Earthquake, Poseidon
'Seismos' they said in the new concrete house

The sea was calm
A hand held flat
The news came over the ship's loudspeaker
Gaddafi…
Casper Weinberger
"What happened?"
"The Americans bomb Libya. Very bad"
"Yes, very bad"
"The tourists not coming"
I should have returned to my household
'Anything that can happen, can happen to you'

In the streets of Vathi wisteria
fills the Venetian ruins swallows
dive under your feet
three military aircraft flew fast and low above me

'the good Odysseus awoke from sleep on his native soil.
After so long an absence, he failed to recognise it; for the
goddess, Pallas Athene, Daughter of Zeus, had thrown a mist
over the place… everything in Ithaca, the long hill-paths,
the quiet bays, the jutting rocks, and the green trees, seemed
unfamiliar…'